MAGNETS

STEVE PARKER

Gareth Stevens Publishing
A WORLD ALMANAC EDUCATION GROUP COMPANY

The original publishers would like to thank the following children from
St. John the Baptist Church of England School and Walnut Tree Walk Primary
School — Danny Bill, Katie Blue, Tony Borg, Stephen Grimshaw, Lauren
Kendrick, Sharday Manahan, Mikki Melaku, Yew Hong Mo, Nickolas Moore,
Louise Morgan, Lola Olayinka, Yemisi Omolewa, Stephen Reid,
Gemma Turland, Joe Westbrook, and Sophie and Alex Lindblom-Smith.
Thanks to Caroline Beattie, the Early Learning Centre, London,
and Broadhurst, Clarkson and Fuller, London.

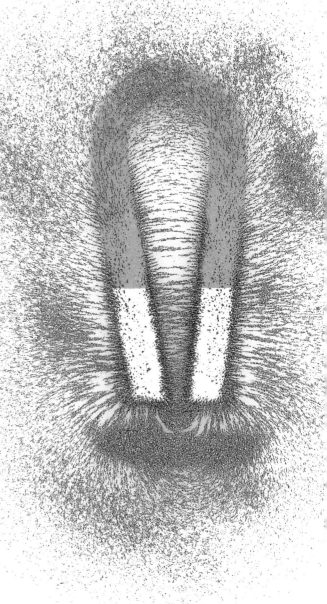

Please visit our web site at: www.garethstevens.com
For a free color catalog describing Gareth Stevens'
list of high-quality books and multimedia programs,
call 1-800-542-2595 (USA) or 1-800-461-9120 (Canada).
Gareth Stevens Publishing's Fax: (414) 332-3567.

Library of Congress Cataloging-in-Publication Data

Parker, Steve.
Magnets / by Steve Parker.
p. cm. — (Young scientist concepts and projects)
Includes bibliographical references and index.
Summary: Describes different kinds of magnets and how
they are used and presents a variety of experiments
and other activities involving magnetism.
ISBN 0-8368-2086-X (lib. bdg.)
1. Magnets—Juvenile literature. 2. Magnets—Experiments—
Juvenile literature. 3. Magnetism—Juvenile literature.
[1. Magnets. 2. Magnetism. 3. Magnets—Experiments.
4. Magnetism—Experiments. 5. Experiments.]
I. Title. II. Series.
QC757.5.P37 1998
538—dc21 97-41625

This North American edition first published in 1998 by
Gareth Stevens Publishing
A World Almanac Education Group Company
330 West Olive Street, Suite 100
Milwaukee, WI 53212 USA

Original edition © 1997 by Anness Publishing Limited.
First published in 1997 by Lorenz Books, an imprint of Anness Publishing Inc.,
New York, New York. This U.S. edition © 1998 by Gareth Stevens, Inc.
Additional end matter © 1998 by Gareth Stevens, Inc.

Editor: Sam Batra
Consultant: Alison Porter, BSc, Science Museum, London
Photographer: John Freeman
Stylists: Thomasina Smith and Isolde Sommerfeldt
Designer: Caroline Reeves
Picture Researcher: Liz Eddison
Illustrator: Kuo Kang Chen
Gareth Stevens series editor: Dorothy L. Gibbs
Editorial assistant: Diane Laska

Printed in the United States of America

3 4 5 6 7 8 9 05 04 03 02 01

YOUNG SCIENTIST CONCEPTS & PROJECTS

MAGNETS

CONTENTS

MAGNETS AND MAGNETISM

Magnets inside colorful plastic cases can hold pieces of paper on metal surfaces such as the refrigerator or washing machine. Enjoy rearranging them as often as you like.

HAVE you used a magnet today? Maybe you stuck a message on the refrigerator door with a magnetic note-holder. Magnets and magnetism are found in many other places, too. Almost any device or machine that has an electric motor uses magnetism – from a cassette deck or CD player to a washing machine or dryer. Countless other types of equipment and machinery in homes, schools, offices, and factories also use magnetism. They include computers, radios, power drills, and even giant electricity-making power stations. Magnetism is a mysterious force that we cannot see. Yet, we live with its effects every day.

Speed
Are there magnets on bicycles? Some bicycles have a speedometer that works with a spinning magnet. If the bicycle's lights are powered by a generator, that also uses magnetism.

Warm and dry
The electric motor in a blow-dryer uses magnetism. It spins a small fan that blows warm air and dries your hair.

Finding the way
Today's boats and ships have satellite navigation systems. However, they still use a magnetic compass to check their route and find their way, just like sailors did hundreds of years ago.

Making music
To create its sound, the electric guitar relies on magnetism to make electrical signals. The guitar is plugged into an electric amplifier so that its sound can be heard.

Flying high
Modern aircraft have magnetic compasses, and their equipment and systems use magnetism. Magnets also operate the autopilot that controls a plane for part of its journey.

WHAT IS A MAGNET?

MAGNETS usually are made of iron or another metal that has lots of iron in it, such as steel. They can be various shapes, big or small, but all magnets have a special ability that seems almost magical. They can pull things toward themselves by an invisible force called magnetism. But a magnet attracts, or pulls, only certain things, mostly things that are made of iron or contain iron.

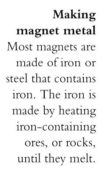

A magnet's power to attract can be transferred through objects. To see this, attach a steel paper clip onto a magnet. Then, hang another paper clip onto the first and repeat to make a chain.

Making magnet metal
Most magnets are made of iron or steel that contains iron. The iron is made by heating iron-containing ores, or rocks, until they melt.

Shape and size
You cannot tell a magnet by its shape or size. It can be a straight bar, a button, a horseshoe, and many other shapes. It may be red, but, if so, it has been painted that way. The red horseshoe *(right)* is a recognizable magnet shape.

Tiny magnets

Think of a bar of iron as having millions of micromagnets, called domains, inside it. If the micromagnets are all mixed up, the bar is not a magnet. If the micromagnets are lined up and point the same way, the bar is a magnet.

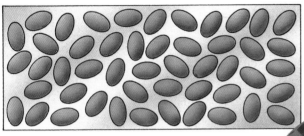

Mixed-up micromagnets — not a magnet.

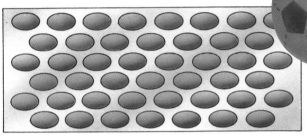

Lined-up micromagnets — a magnet.

FACT BOX

• You cannot tell if something is a magnet by looking at its shape, size, or color. You need to test it with objects that contain iron.

• Ordinary types of magnets are called permanent magnets. They are magnetic all the time, and they keep their magnetism for months and years. There are other kinds of magnets, such as electromagnets, whose strength and magnetism vary.

• Every magnet has two poles, or ends, no matter what shape it is.

• Most metals are not magnetic. The most common magnetic metals are cobalt, nickel, and iron.

Atoms

The tiny domains, or micromagnets, inside iron are actually groups of atoms. All materials – metals, nonmetals, gases, and liquids – are made from atoms, which are so small that even the most powerful microscopes cannot see them. Atoms spin around just like a ball balanced on the top of your finger.

7

MAKING MAGNETS

A simple horseshoe magnet is a familiar but fascinating object.

Y ou can make your own magnet from a rod, strip, or bar of something made of iron or steel that is not already a magnet. To do this, you also need a real magnet. Steel is mostly iron and usually works well. There are many suitable items, from screws to screwdrivers. Try some objects that are made from different metals, such as brass or aluminum, or from other substances, such as wood, plastic, or paper. See what you find when experimenting with these other materials in comparison with those made from iron or steel.

M A T E R I A L S

You will need: iron nail, magnet, paper clips, brass pin.

Make your own magnet

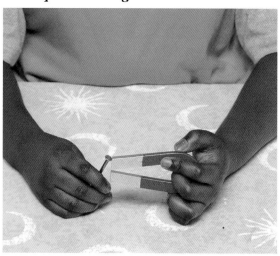

Take an iron nail and stroke it about 50 times with one end of a magnet. Stroke it along its length from one end to the other. The nail is now a magnet itself. Can it pick up paper clips or a brass pin?

Movement of pole of horseshoe magnet

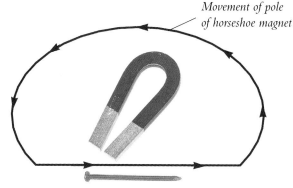

This diagram shows how to move the magnet when stroking the nail. Remember to always use the same pole, to move in the same direction, and to lift the magnet clear after each stroke.

Does it stick?
Objects made of brass or other metals, apart from iron or steel, usually cannot be made into magnets. Do they even stick to a real magnet?

Ruining a magnet
Use the iron nail that you have made into a magnet. Tap it hard several times with the hammer. This shakes up all the tiny micromagnets inside and destroys the magnetism.

M A T E R I A L S

You will need: brass screw, magnet, iron nail, hammer, empty aluminum soda can, paper clip.

No stick, no magnet
The soda can is aluminum. It does not stick to a real magnet. You cannot make it into a magnet by stroking either – no matter how long you try!

Testing magnets
The usual test for a magnet is to try to pick up something made of iron or steel. If an iron nail is too heavy for a weak magnet, try a shiny steel paper clip instead.

HISTORY OF MAGNETS

PEOPLE have known about magnets and magnetism for thousands of years, because some magnets occur naturally. In certain places, you can pick them up from the ground. These natural magnets are usually lumps of stone called lodestone or magnetite, a type of rock that contains lots of iron. Ancient peoples noticed that two lumps of this rock sometimes tried to stick together or push each other apart. Then, sailors and explorers discovered how to use thin slivers of this rock as magnetic compasses to find their way. However, people have understood more about magnets only in the last 200 years.

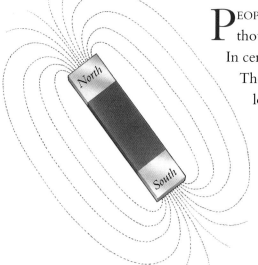

A typical bar magnet has two ends called poles. The invisible magnetism, called lines of magnetic force, is strongest around these ends.

The compass
About 1,000 years ago, sailors and explorers made a discovery. They found that a thin piece of lodestone, floating freely in a bowl of water, always would point the same way – north and south. They had discovered the magnetic compass.

Magnetic rock
Lodestone, also called magnetite, is a natural magnet. Dig it out of the ground, and iron-containing objects, such as nails and pins, stick to it – just as they do to manufactured magnets.

Compass on board

During the great days of sailing ships, the magnetic compass was a vital piece of equipment. It showed which way was north, south, east, or west. The navigator used the compass and maps to follow the ship's position.

Better compasses

In the 1600s, compasses were being made using strips of magnetized iron that were allowed to twirl around freely. The compass was put in an elegant, portable box that was decorated with attractive designs and patterns.

The fabled land

Some adventurers suggested that the North Pole was a paradise bathed in sunlight, warmth, and peace. Others wanted to discover new trade routes by finding a shortcut to the East around the top of North America. But their ships got trapped, their camps froze, and many explorers died. The *magnetic* north pole first was reached by British explorer James Ross and his expedition in 1861.

FACT BOX

• The name *magnet* may come from Magnesia. This was a region in Thessaly in ancient Greece. A part of modern Greece in the same area is called Magnisia.

• More than 2,500 years ago, the ancient Greeks knew about the mysterious powers of the rock called lodestone.

• No one is sure who invented the first magnetic compass. It may have been the ancient Chinese, about 1,800 years ago. By the year A.D. 1000, the Chinese were using compasses to find their way at sea.

• By the 1100s, the use of compasses had spread as far as the Middle East and Europe.

WHAT DO MAGNETS ATTRACT?

The human body has tiny amounts of iron in the blood but too little to be affected by a magnet.

Most ordinary magnets attract only certain objects, things containing the metal iron. So, how can you tell if an object is made of iron or contains iron? Try testing it with a magnet. For some objects, the attraction is very weak, so you have to test them carefully and feel for the pulling force. For other objects, the attraction is strong enough to make the objects stick to the magnet. Remember that it is the magnet that does the pulling, not the object – unless that is a magnet, too!

Cans

A soda can is probably made of aluminum, which is a metal, but it is not iron. The magnet does not pull or attract it. You could try an empty food can, such as one used for baked beans or soup. What happens then?

MATERIALS

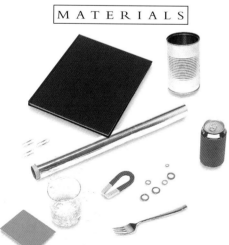

You will need: magnet, aluminum soda can, empty food can, glass or plastic beaker, stainless steel fork, book, paper, card, paper clip, metal washers, aluminum foil.

WARNING
Be very careful when testing sharp objects,
such as needles, nails, cans, and pins. Do not
hang breakable objects on a magnet. A sudden
jolt might make them fall to the floor!

Paper products
Try the magnetic test on a book or
a sheet of paper. Does the magnet
attract them? Can the magnetism
attract a paper clip? Will it pass
through the book or paper?
Try different thicknesses of
these materials and write
down your results.

Glass and plastic
Try the glass to see if the magnet
attracts it. Glass and plastic do
not contain iron, so they are not
magnetic. See if the magnetism
can pass through
the glass by
holding the
magnet on
the outside
and putting
a fork on
the inside.

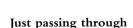

Just passing through
Test metal washers
with a magnet. They
probably are steel, so
they are attracted to
it. Test foil, too.
It probably is
aluminum, so it is
not attracted. Now
test the washers with
the foil between them
and the magnet. Does
the magnetism pass
through the foil?

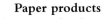

13

POLES APART

The two poles of some magnets, such as this bar magnet (left), are colored or labeled — usually red, or N, for north. Another color, sometimes blue, may represent S for south.

THE two poles, or ends, of a magnet may look the same, but they are not. Put one pole of a magnet near a pole of another magnet to find out the differences. You may feel an attraction force, or pulling, and the two poles stick together strongly. Alternatively, you may feel a repulsion force, or pushing, as the two poles twist and repel each other. The different poles are called the north pole and the south pole. In all magnets, two identical poles will push each other away, while two different poles will pull toward each other. These are basic features of all magnets.

Like poles repel
Like poles repel, unlike poles attract. This saying helps people remember a vital feature of magnets. It means that the same poles of two different magnets will repel, or push each other apart. Put two north poles together, and they repel. Two south poles also repel.

Unlike poles attract
The poles of two magnets that are different, or opposite, will attract. Put a north pole and south pole together, and they will attract.

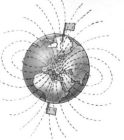

North and south
Why are a magnet's poles called north and south? This is because the north pole points to the magnetic north pole in the Arctic Ocean at the top of the world. The south pole points to the magnetic south pole on Antarctica. Their full names are north-seeking pole and south-seeking pole.

Poles and shapes
Magnetism is concentrated around the poles of a magnet. In the note-holder magnets *(above)*, each pole is on an opposite side of the disk. This is why the magnet sticks to the refrigerator on its side.

Push-up train
Some trains have no wheels. Instead, there are magnets in the base of the train and magnetism in the track. The like poles face each other, so they repel, lifting the train so it floats by magnetic repulsion, called magnetic levitation, or maglev.

SEEING MAGNETISM

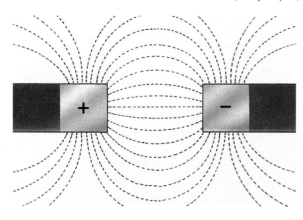

YOU cannot see the magnetic force around a magnet, but you can see the effects of its presence when an iron nail sticks to a magnet. You can see the shape and extent of a magnetic field by using tiny, powder-like pieces of iron called iron filings. Magnetism makes them move and line up. More than 150 years ago, British scientist Michael Faraday studied magnets using iron filings. He noticed that the iron filings were attracted to lines of magnetic force. Today, diagrams are drawn to show that magnetism is made up of lines of magnetic force. The north pole has a + sign (positive or plus) and the south pole a - sign (negative or minus).

You cannot see magnetic lines of force. You cannot feel, hear, smell, or taste them. People need to use magnetic objects, such as paper clips, iron filings, or a compass, to see how strong a magnetic force is.

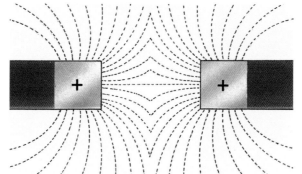

Repulsion force
Magnetic lines of force from the like poles of two magnets push against each other strongly. They can be north and north or south and south.

Attraction force
Magnetic lines of force from unlike poles, north and south, join and pull together powerfully. The attracting force is stronger than one magnet pulling on an ordinary iron object, such as a nail.

Ring magnet
Iron filings are tiny and light. They can move to line up with the magnetic force, and they cluster where it is strongest. They show that this ring magnet has one pole on the inside of the ring and the other around the outside.

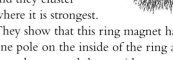

Compasses and magnetic fields

A magnetic compass usually lines up with the earth's weak magnetism. Place a strong magnet nearby, and you can overpower the earth's magnetism and make the compass needle line up with the magnet. The north end of the compass points toward the magnet's north pole. The compass's south end points to the magnet's south pole. The whole area of magnetism around any magnet, as shown by the lines of magnetic force, is called its magnetic field. Stronger magnets have larger magnetic fields. The power of the magnetic field fades as it gets farther from its magnet.

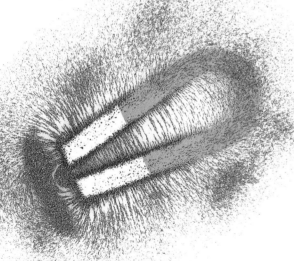

Compass points follow lines of magnetic force from a nearby bar magnet.

Bar magnet

Iron filings line up to show how the magnetic force spreads out from the poles, or ends, of the bar. The tiny particles of filings are magnetic, but not magnetized, as they do not show the difference between north and south poles.

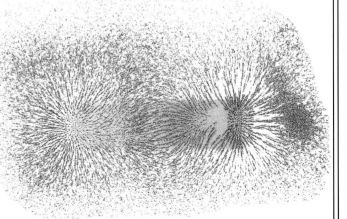

Horseshoe magnet

Iron filings reveal that the lines and strength of the magnetic force are concentrated around and between the poles at the ends of the horseshoe. There is little magnetism on the curved main body of the magnet because it is farther away from the poles.

PUSH AND PULL

You will need:
scissors, double-sided tape,
round plastic container,
2 magnets, rubber bands,
3 steel washers, 2 rulers.

Is a big magnet more powerful than a small one? Not necessarily. You cannot tell how powerful a magnet is by just looking at it. A magnet that is smaller than a matchbook can be stronger than one bigger than a brick. It depends on exactly what the magnet is made of and how it is first given its magnetism, or how it has been magnetized. Every year, vast amounts of money are spent on research into new combinations of metals to make magnets that are smaller, lighter, and stronger than their predecessors. These metal combinations are called alloys. Steel, made from iron and carbon, is a common example. This simple magnet strength-tester compares the power of different magnets.

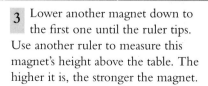

Strength of a magnet

1 Cut off a length of double-sided tape and use it to attach the round container firmly to the work surface. The container will act as the pivot, or the balancer.

2 Attach a magnet to one end of the ruler with a rubber band and attach some washers to the other end. Position the middle of the ruler on the balancer.

3 Lower another magnet down to the first one until the ruler tips. Use another ruler to measure this magnet's height above the table. The higher it is, the stronger the magnet.

Power of a magnet

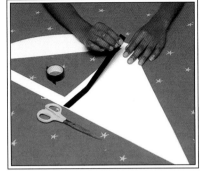

1 Attach thread to a drawing pin and a pencil, or use a pair of compasses, to draw two quarter-circles on cardboard that are a ruler's length from the center to the edge.

2 Draw a triangle in one quarter-circle and cut it out. Make a triangle from the second quarter-circle. Tape the two together, *as shown above*.

3 Push a drawing pin through the hole at the end of the ruler so that it pivots. Attach rubber bands from the hole in the middle of the ruler to the side of the quarter-circle, *as shown above*. Add stick-on dots to each end of the ruler and label them *N* and *S*.

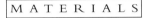

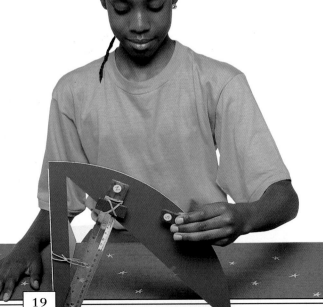

You will need: *thread, drawing pins, pencil, pair of compasses, cardboard, scissors, tape, ruler with 2 holes in it, rubber bands, stick-on dots, pen, magnets.*

4 Stand the magnet-measurer upright. Attach one magnet to the top end of the ruler with a rubber band. Bring the unlike or opposite pole of another magnet near it. How far can it pull the ruler? Stronger magnets pull it farther.

MAGNETS AND THEIR USES

MAGNETS are more complicated than they might seem at first. There are different shapes and sizes with different strengths of magnetic fields. They have north and south poles that attract or repel. These features make magnets very useful. They are found in hundreds of tools, toys, machines, and gadgets, from small magnets on cabinet door catches to giant magnets in the motors of electric trains. The magnets used in these gadgets are permanent magnets. Their magnetism lasts for years and can be used in many different ways. How many things containing magnets do you notice around your home?

Each of the brightly colored plastic letters and numbers has a small magnet inside it. The magnet sticks to the white board because the board is a thin sheet of material containing iron.

Magnetic disk

Out of its protective case, a computer disk looks like a dark plastic circle. It has a thin, iron-based coating that can hold millions of bits of information as microscopic patches of magnetism.

Magnetic motor

Almost anything with an electric motor has a magnet, because magnetism is how the motor turns around. This includes electric drills, screwdrivers, and similar tools, whether they use batteries for power or the electricity supply from a wall socket.

Magnetic can opener

Some can openers have a magnet in an arm that touches the top of the can. As the can is opened, the lid stays attached to the magnet, so you are less likely to cut yourself on its sharp edge. These cans are made of steel coated with tin.

Magnetic holder

A magnet can attract and hold small iron or steel objects such as paper clips, drawing pins, sewing needles, and dressmaking pins. This container *(right)* is designed to hold paper clips or pins and has a magnetic lid to attract them. If you accidentally drop them all over the floor, sweeping the magnetic lid over them helps pick them up again.

FACT BOX

• Magnets often are used in recycling. They are used to single out cans that contain iron or iron alloys from those that are made of aluminum.

• Refrigerator doors have magnetic strips around their edges. When the door is closed, the magnetic strip sticks to the refrigerator, keeping the door firmly in place to stop warm air from getting inside and spoiling the food.

• Magnets prevent damage to motor engines. As oil passes through the engine's mechanism, it picks up tiny bits of steel that are being worn away. Special magnetic plugs pick up these bits of steel and wash them into the sump, a container for the oil.

Magnetic screwdriver

Some manual screwdrivers are magnetic. The steel shaft is a long bar magnet that helps small steel screws stick to the end as you use them. You also can use the screwdriver to lift small iron-containing objects out of odd places.

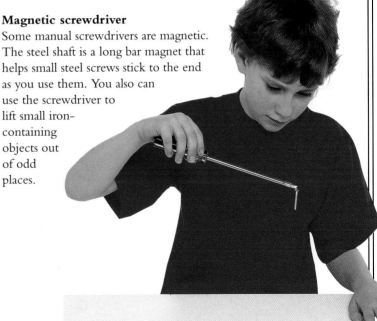

MAGNETIC FISHING

MAGNETS on lines or ropes can be used to fish iron-containing objects out of awkward places. Salvage crews, for example, use huge magnets to recover pieces of wrecked ships and other equipment from the seabed. The magnets are used where the locations are dangerous, or in murky water, mud, and dark holes where the items cannot be seen or reached without difficulty. The magnetic fishing game *(below)* demonstrates how magnets are used in such a way.

This is a powerful example of how much strength a magnet can have. This magnet was displayed at a technological exhibition in London in the 1920s.

M A T E R I A L S

You will need: different colored plastic bags, felt-tip marker, scissors, paper clips, 2 magnets, string, 2 wooden dowels, tape, deep plate or shallow bowl, watering can, water.

Fishing to win

1 Draw some fish shapes on the colored plastic bags with the felt-tip marker. Cut out the shapes carefully with the scissors.

2 Decorate the fish. Draw scales with the marker on one side and write a number on the other side. Give the fish different numbers.

3 Firmly attach a steel paper clip to each fish. The paper clip will allow you to catch the fish with a magnetic rod.

4 Tie each magnet to one end of a piece of string. If you tie the string around the middle of the magnet, it will be secure.

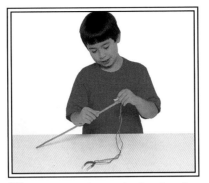

5 Tape the other end of each string to the end of a wooden dowel. Make sure it is taped securely.

6 Put your fish, scale side up, in the plate or bowl. Fill the plate or bowl with water. You are now ready to start the fishing game.

WARNING
Keep plastic bags away from small children because these bags can be very dangerous.

Playing the fishing game
Each player dangles a fishing pole over the plate or bowl. When one of the players says "go," lower your fishing pole into the water to catch the fish. The steel paper clips on the fish will be attracted to the magnet on the end of your pole. Carefully lift your fish out of the pond. Each player can make his or her own pile of fish. When there are no fish left in the pond, each player adds his or her points (from the back of the fish) together. The highest score wins.

THE BIGGEST MAGNET

W HAT is the biggest magnet in the world? You are sitting or standing on it right now. It *is* the world! Planet Earth is like a giant magnet. However, its magnetism is weak. We usually do not notice it except when magnetic compasses detect it and find north and south. Then, the earth's magnetism is very useful. The force that pulls things down to the center of the earth and makes them fall to the ground is not magnetism. It is called gravity. It affects everything, whether magnetic or not.

Think of earth as a giant magnet spinning through space. Its lines of magnetic force extend into space.

The iron core

How does the earth make its magnetism? Scientists believe it may be due to electric currents flowing in the core, the huge and solid center of the planet. The core is made mostly of iron and nickel, which is under enormous pressure and at a very high temperature. The flowing movements may create the magnetism, like a huge bar magnet inside the world.

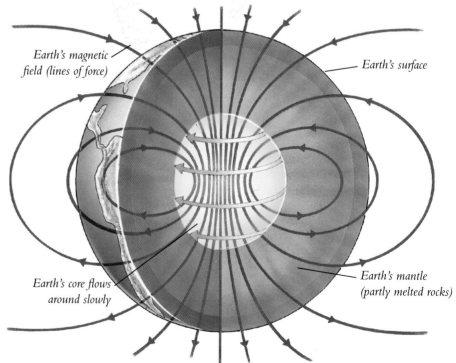

Earth's magnetic field (lines of force)

Earth's surface

Earth's core flows around slowly

Earth's mantle (partly melted rocks)

Warm winds and sun

Winds that blow up from the south to Europe bring warm, dry air from the Sahara Desert region of North Africa. Sometimes wind is described by the direction from which it is blowing. The name of this direction comes from the names of earth's magnetic poles. Easterly and westerly winds come from directions at right angles to the north and south poles.

Magnetic storms

Some types of storms and thunderclouds have immense amounts of magnetism and electricity in them, much stronger than earth's normal magnetic field. They are called magnetic storms. They can affect radio and television sets by disturbing the radio waves that the sets pick up.

Cold winds and snow

"The north wind doth blow, and we shall have snow," goes the rhyme. Winds blowing from a certain direction usually bring certain kinds of weather. In Europe and North America, winds from the north bring cold air, frost, and snow down from the north pole and arctic region.

HOW A COMPASS WORKS

You will need: paper clip, strong magnet, tape, piece of cork tile, deep plate or shallow bowl, water, ready-made compass.

IF you were a sailor or an explorer setting off on an exciting journey into unknown lands, one of the most important things you could have would be a compass. The compass needle is a simple magnet. It is long and thin so that it can spin freely around on a pivot. This simple instrument has saved countless lives, from people lost in the jungle or desert to sailors cast adrift at sea. It has many useful features, even compared with modern devices such as electronic satellite navigation equipment that uses the Global Positioning System (GPS). The magnetic compass is small, simple, and reliable. It needs no batteries or fuel. Used correctly, it is very accurate. When looked after properly, a good compass should last a lifetime.

Making a simple compass

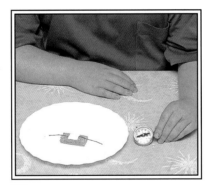

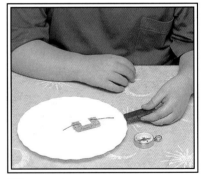

1 Straighten out a paper clip. Stroke it about 50 times (always in the same direction) with one pole of a magnet. Tape the paper clip (now a magnet) to a piece of cork. Float the cork in a plate or bowl of water.

2 The paper clip magnet should point north and south. Its north pole is attracted to earth's North Pole. Compare it with a ready-made compass. Is your paper clip compass accurate?

3 If you bring a strong magnet near a compass, its magnetic field overpowers the earth's magnetic field. It attracts the compass, which now lines up with the nearby magnet.

Using a compass

To use a ready-made compass, hold it level and steady so the needle can spin freely. Let it settle and note where it points. Do this several times to be sure that the needle does not stick on the base or on its pivot. Carefully turn the base so the N, or north, lines up with the needle. The base usually has a spot of paint or an N to indicate its north-seeking end. Compare your homemade paper clip compass with the ready-made one. Remember that a compass needle or pointer is a magnet. What happens if you put your homemade paper clip compass very near the ready-made compass needle? Do they swing around to point at each other? They may, since their unlike poles will attract each other while the like poles repel.

M A T E R I A L S

You will need: paper clip, strong magnet, cardboard, scissors, thin wire, piece of cork tile, tape, thread, ready-made compass.

Making a loop compass

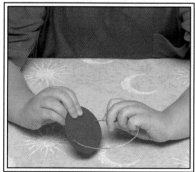

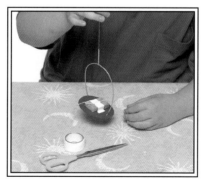

1 Straighten out a paper clip. Magnetize it by stroking it with the strong magnet. Cut out a disk of cardboard. Bend some wire into a large loop and insert it into the disk.

2 Tape the paper clip to the piece of cork, and tape both to the cardboard disk. Tie thread at the top of the wire loop. Let the loop compass hang and twirl freely.

3 Does the paper clip magnet work like a compass needle and point north and south? Check it with the ready-made compass. What do you find?

THE MAGNETIC POLES

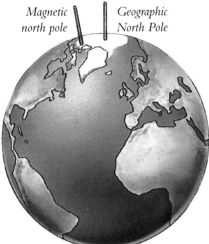

Magnetic north pole   Geographic North Pole

Geographic South Pole   Magnetic south pole

The geographic poles indicate earth's axis, the imaginary line around which it spins in space. The magnetic poles show where earth's magnetism is concentrated.

A polar gap

Due to the way earth's magnetic field is generated, the direction of earth's magnetism is at a slight angle to earth's axis. The magnetic north pole is among the islands of northern North America, several hundred miles (kilometers) from the geographic North Pole in the Arctic Ocean. A compass needle points to the magnetic north pole.

T HE earth is like a giant magnet – so it must have two poles. We call them the magnetic north pole and the magnetic south pole. There is, however, another pair of poles – the geographic North Pole and the geographic South Pole. They are in different places from their matching magnetic poles. The magnetic poles are where a compass points. The geographic poles mark the line, or axis, around which the earth spins. The areas around the poles are called the polar regions. They are at the top and bottom of the world, where the sun is very weak – so it is very cold there.

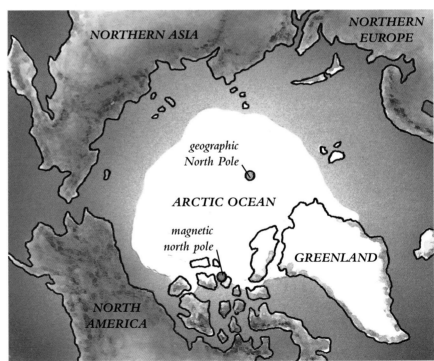

NORTHERN ASIA

NORTHERN EUROPE

geographic North Pole

ARCTIC OCEAN

magnetic north pole

GREENLAND

NORTH AMERICA

Race to the North Pole

The geographic North Pole is in the middle of the Arctic Ocean, which is always covered with a layer of ice. The first explorer to walk across the dangerous, shifting icecap was probably American Robert Peary in 1909 *(left)*. However, some experts say that he failed to reach the North Pole.

FACT BOX

• The magnetic north and south poles do not stay still. Over hundreds and thousands of years, they drift.

• Sometimes magnetic north and south switch, so the magnetic north pole is suddenly near the geographic South Pole, and the magnetic south pole is near the geographic North Pole! This is called a magnetic reversal. It has happened hundreds of times over millions of years.

• As certain kinds of rocks form on the earth, magnetism is trapped inside them like billions of tiny compass needles. Rocks of different ages show how the magnetic poles have moved and switched.

Fossil ferns in the snow
The land near the North Pole is now snow-covered. Millions of years ago, it was warm, and plants flourished.

Race to the South Pole

The geographic South Pole is on the great southern continent of Antarctica, which is completely covered with thick ice most of the year. In 1911, two teams of explorers raced to get there. Norwegian Roald Amundsen's group was first and returned safely. British Robert Falcon Scott's (*right*) expedition arrived one month later. On arrival, they found a sympathetic note from Amundsen. Sadly, Scott and his men did not survive the return journey.

MAGNETS IN SPACE

THE earth's magnetism is not just on the ground, where it is detected with compasses. Like any other magnet, earth's magnetic field extends away from it, into the air – even into space. But the magnetic field is not equal on both sides of the planet, as it is with most ordinary magnets. A stream of energy and particles from the sun, called solar wind, blows through the magnetic field and makes it lopsided. This vast region, where the magnetic field meets the solar wind, is called the magnetosphere. It extends thousands of miles (kilometers) into space, especially on the night side of earth, the side away from the sun.

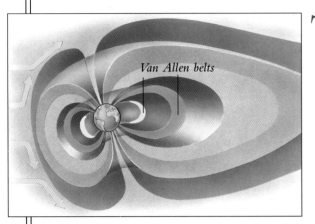

The magnetosphere is the region in space around the earth where solar wind from the sun blows through the earth's magnetic field. It is like a giant lopsided doughnut. It has several layers, including the Van Allen belts, named after the scientist who discovered them from satellite information.

Van Allen belts

Magnetism in deep space

Powerful telescopes and satellite equipment show that there is magnetism deep in space. It usually is concentrated around incredibly vast objects such as galaxies and quasars. The magnetism is powerful, billions of times stronger than any magnets made on earth.

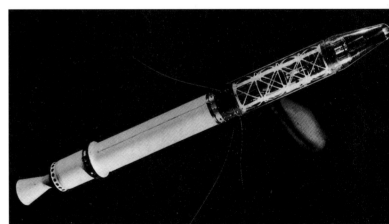

Finding the field

In 1958, one of earth's first satellites, *Explorer 1*, detected magnetic layers around earth. In the early 1960s, *Explorer 12* proved that the magnetosphere existed. Its scientific instruments detected the magnetism and energy far into space.

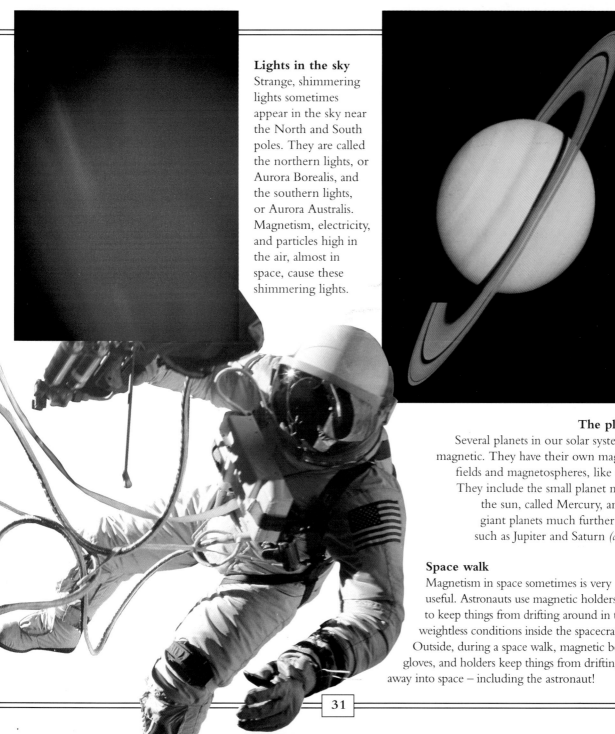

Lights in the sky
Strange, shimmering lights sometimes appear in the sky near the North and South poles. They are called the northern lights, or Aurora Borealis, and the southern lights, or Aurora Australis. Magnetism, electricity, and particles high in the air, almost in space, cause these shimmering lights.

The planets
Several planets in our solar system are magnetic. They have their own magnetic fields and magnetospheres, like earth. They include the small planet nearest the sun, called Mercury, and the giant planets much further away, such as Jupiter and Saturn *(above)*.

Space walk
Magnetism in space sometimes is very useful. Astronauts use magnetic holders to keep things from drifting around in the weightless conditions inside the spacecraft. Outside, during a space walk, magnetic boots, gloves, and holders keep things from drifting away into space – including the astronaut!

MAGNETS AND MAPS

Look at a map – which way is up? Maps are made according to earth's magnetism and the magnetic compass. They have north at the top, in the same way that the North Pole is at the top of the world. We are used to looking at maps and using them with north at the top, pointing straight up or away from us. Look on a local map to find a diagram of the compass points and an arrow or N that indicates north. Then, using a compass, turn the map so its north faces the same way as the compass north. Now the map is lined up accurately in relation to the landscape. If you are on a hilltop with wide views, you can see how the map is a tiny version of the countryside all around.

Maps are important. They let us know our location. Without magnets, we would not know how to use a map or find our way around an area.

Which way is up?
We are so familiar with maps having north at the top that they look odd when they are turned around. Can you recognize this country *(left)* when it is turned upside down? Can you find it on the globe *(right)*?

The compass maze

Can you find your way through this maze? When you have made it to the other side, try recording your route with compass points. At the beginning of the journey, you head east, turn north, and then go east again. Can you complete these instructions for the entire journey?

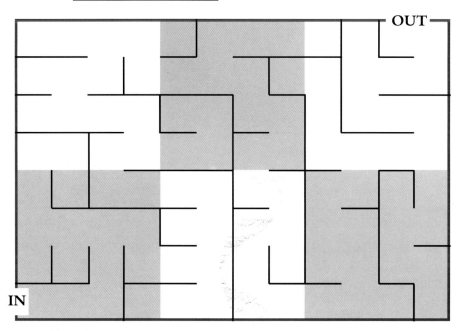

OUT

IN

Drawing a maze

You will need: cardboard, colored markers, compass.

1 Draw your own maze. Make it colorful and fun. Put in some dead ends and false turns. Make sure one route leads all the way through from one end of the maze to the other – even though it may be very twisty!

2 Record your course through the maze using compass points for the directions. You can limit the information to north, south, east, and west, or include more detailed directions such as northeast and southwest.

MAGNETIC SENSE

Magnetism is probably an important guide to the arctic tern on its migratory route. It flies to the far north for the summer. To avoid the long northern winter, it flies around the world to the far south, even to Antarctica.

WE cannot detect magnets or magnetic fields with our own bodies. Various animals, however, seem to sense magnetism. They may detect the earth's magnetic field and use it to help them navigate or find their way on very long journeys called migrations. Like human sailors or explorers using a magnetic compass, these animals seem to have a built-in body compass. Many kinds of animals migrate. They include swallows, geese, and various other birds; fish, such as salmon; and large mammals, such as whales, seals, and caribou. Scientists have not yet discovered where this natural compass is in the animal's body or exactly how it works.

Whales at sea

Many great whales and other types of sea mammals go on long, annual journeys. They usually start from their winter areas of warm tropical seas and move to their summer areas of polar seas, where food is plentiful. Like other migrating sea animals, they probably use several clues to find their way, such as coastlines, undersea mountains or cliffs, sea currents, the earth's gravity, and magnetism.

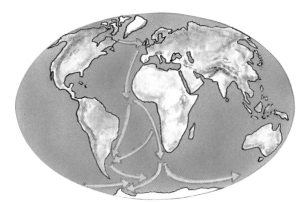

Migration route

The tern's migration follows the earth's lines of magnetic force. It flies from north to south and then returns later in the year, from south to north. Birds probably use several clues to navigate, such as rivers, mountains, coastlines, the positions of the sun, moon, stars – and magnetism.

Turtle travelers

Sea turtles wander the world's oceans, yet they return to the beach where they hatched from eggs to lay their own eggs.

To the north

The usual reason for migration is to travel to a place where conditions are good for a limited time. In the short arctic summer, plants grow quickly and plentifully. Birds, such as geese, fly there to breed. Insects, such as the monarch butterfly, also go on long annual migrations.

Where is the body compass?

Experiments with pigeons show that they probably use magnetism to navigate. When scientists strapped a small but strong magnet to a pigeon's head, it interfered with the earth's magnetic field – and the pigeon lost its way! A bird's own body compass may be somewhere inside its head, near or inside the brain.

ELECTRIC MAGNETS

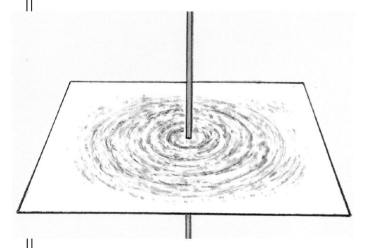

The magnetic field around a wire with electricity flowing through it can be made stronger by wrapping the wire in a coil around an iron bar. The iron bar then works like a bar magnet – but only while electricity flows. This simple device, the electromagnet, is a magnet you can switch on and off. Electromagnets are found by the millions in all kinds of machinery.

THE ordinary bar and horseshoe magnets are permanent magnets. They have what scientists call spontaneous permanent magnetism. Their magnetism needs no outside force or energy. But there is another way of making magnetism – by electricity. When electricity flows through a wire, or a similar conductor (an electricity-carrier), it produces a magnetic field around the wire. This is called electromagnetism, or EM. In fact, magnetism and electricity are very closely linked. Each can be used to make the other. EM is used in thousands of kinds of tools, machines, and devices that are vital in our modern world.

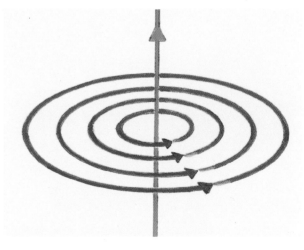

Seeing electromagnetism
If iron filings are sprinkled onto a piece of cardboard that has an electricity-carrying wire through it, the filings are affected by the magnetic field. They arrange themselves in circles to show the lines of magnetic force, as they do with an ordinary magnet.

Creating a magnetic field
As electricity flows through a wire, a magnetic field is created around it. The magnetic lines of force flow in circles around the wire. This is called an electromagnetic field. As soon as the electricity is switched off, the magnetism stops.

EM in toys

Many toys have electromagnets inside them. A battery-operated car steers by using two electromagnets at the front. One twists the wheels so the car steers to the left, and the other makes it go to the right. With both of the electromagnets switched off, a spring pulls the wheels so the car goes straight.

FACT BOX

• In Denmark, in 1820, the scientist Hans Christian Oersted (1777-1851) first discovered that electric current produced magnetism.

• In France, André Marie Ampère (1775-1836) did many experiments on electricity and magnetism. He invented the idea of twisting wire into a coil, called a solenoid, to make its magnetism stronger.

• In England, Michael Faraday (1791-1867) discovered electromagnetic induction, using magnetism to generate an electric current. This discovery led to many useful inventions, including the electric motor, dynamo, and transformer.

• In the United States, Joseph Henry (1797-1878) discovered electromagnetic induction. He made incredibly powerful electromagnets that lifted weights of over a ton.

Switch on and off

One of the most useful features of an electromagnet is that you can switch it on and off. Large electromagnets are strong enough to pick up old cars by their steel roofs and drop them into crushers. Many machines and other types of equipment rely on electromagnets for their effectiveness.

MAKING AN ELECTROMAGNET

THE magnetism of an electromagnet is the same as magnetism from an ordinary magnet. The way of making it differs. The first practical, useful electromagnets were made by British bootmaker and part-time scientist William Sturgeon, in the 1820s, to amaze audiences at his science shows. The basic design has hardly changed since. You can make a similar electromagnet and amaze your friends, too!

You will need: wirestrippers; two yards (meters) of wire (insulated, plastic-coated, multistrand copper); large iron nail, bar, or rod; 9-volt battery; paper clips; piece of cardboard; 2 brass fasteners.

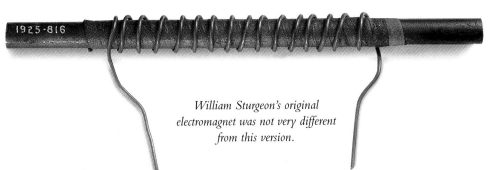

1925-816

William Sturgeon's original electromagnet was not very different from this version.

Your own electromagnet

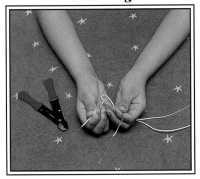

1 Using the wirestrippers, carefully remove a few inches of plastic coating, or insulation, from each end of the wire. These bare ends will connect to the battery.

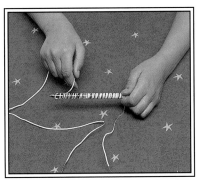

2 Carefully wrap the wire in a tight coil around the iron nail. The insulation around the wire conducts the electricity around the nail.

3 Connect the ends of the wire to the battery terminals. (It does not matter which is positive or negative.) Test your electromagnet by picking up paper clips.

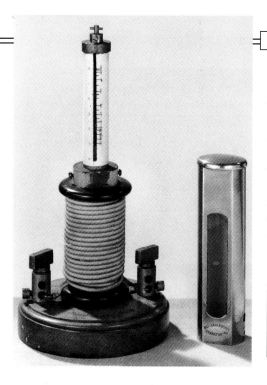

Stronger magnets

This electromagnet *(left)* has two sets of coils, one on top of the other, but both are made from one length of wire. There are several ways of making an electromagnet stronger and more powerful. One is to put more turns of wire onto the central iron rod or bar. You could try making your own version of this electromagnet with a longer piece of wire. Wrap one set of turns around the nail. Then make another set of turns to form a second coil on top of the first. Another way is to use more electricity, such as two 9-volt batteries. In this project, electricity flows as soon as the wires are joined to the battery. This quickly can run down the battery. It is better to have a switch, so you can turn the electromagnet on and off easily, as needed.

WARNING

NEVER try using electricity from wall sockets. It is far too dangerous and could kill you. Ask an adult for help with this project.

Adding a switch

1 Make two equal-size holes in the piece of cardboard. Push the brass fasteners into them. Push one of the brass fasteners through a paper clip first. Open the prongs of the brass fastener. Each prong now is ready to connect to the wire.

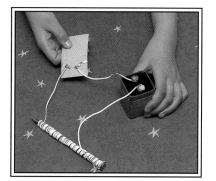

2 Connect one end of the electromagnet wire to a brass fastener. Connect the other end to a battery terminal. Attach the other brass fastener to the other battery terminal with another short piece of wire. Turn the cardboard over.

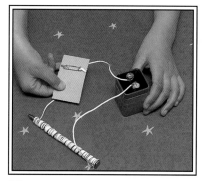

3 The paper clip attached to one brass fastener is the switch. Push it away from the other brass fastener. Notice that no electricity flows. If you turn the paper clip to touch the other brass fastener, electricity flows and switches on the electromagnet.

EM MACHINES

Hundreds of machines use the switchable on-off magnetic power of electromagnetism. You can find them around your home, at school, in factories and offices, in the car, and at the supermarket – just about everywhere. Some electromagnetic machines use electricity from batteries. Others need the much more powerful electricity from wall sockets.

A metal detector uses electromagnetism to signal if iron-containing substances are nearby. Some detectors also can locate other types of metals. They work by battery power.

Medical scanners

The magnetic resonance imager (MRI) is a type of scanner that can see inside the body. The person is put into a huge electromagnet, which uses a combination of magnetism and radio waves to detect different parts inside the body. A computer processes the results and shows them on a screen.

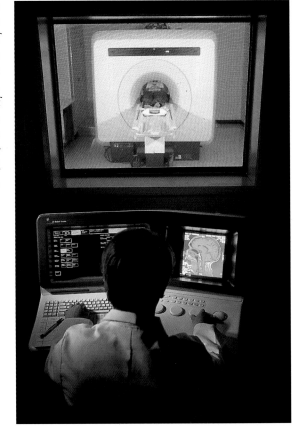

Recycling

At some recycling centers, aluminum soda cans and steel food cans all go into the same container. At the recycling plant, an electromagnet separates them by attracting the steel cans but not the aluminum ones.

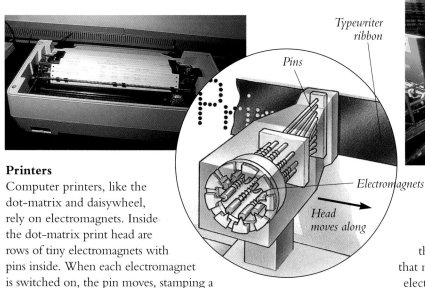

Typewriter ribbon

Pins

Electromagnets

Head moves along

Printers

Computer printers, like the dot–matrix and daisywheel, rely on electromagnets. Inside the dot-matrix print head are rows of tiny electromagnets with pins inside. When each electromagnet is switched on, the pin moves, stamping a tiny dot on the paper with the ink ribbon. This movement occurs hundreds of times each second.

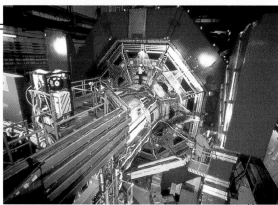

Smashing atoms

The biggest machines in the world are giant atom-smashers, such as particle accelerators and colliders. Scientists use them to study the inner workings of atoms that make up everything in the universe. Large electromagnets affect the tiniest bits of atomic particles, such as electrons and protons, making them surge through the tubes at incredible speeds and smash together.

Making televisions

These workers are putting together televisions in a factory in Japan. Magnets are an important part of the electrical circuits found in a television set.

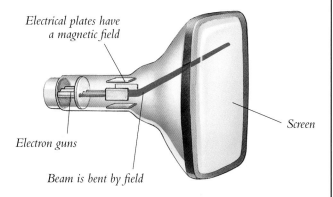

Electrical plates have a magnetic field

Screen

Electron guns

Beam is bent by field

Inside the television

Television sets, computer monitors, and similar screens have electromagnet-type devices inside. They usually are shaped like flat plates. They bend the beam that scans across the screen, line-by-line, to build up the picture. This action occurs many times each second.

THE EM OLYMPICS

ELECTROMAGNETS are found in many toys and games. You can use the power of electromagnetism to make your own game, the EM Olympics. Here, a metal washer represents a discus, a nut is a shot put, and a nail is a javelin. The electromagnet is used to throw each of them. The secret of success is timing. At the exact moment you switch off the electromagnet, it stops attracting the iron or steel object and releases it.

Throwing a real javelin is one of several Olympic field events (right). The sport probably began in ancient times with spears.

M A T E R I A L S

You will need: sheets of cardboard, scissors, glue, tape, marker pen, decorative stick-on shapes, large iron nail, insulated (plastic-coated) copper wire, wirestrippers, battery, paper clip, brass fasteners, small nail, metal washer, nut.

The EM games

1 Cut a cardboard base 15-20 inches (38-50 cm) long and wide. Cut four sides the same length and 4-6 inches (10-15 cm) deep. Glue the base and sides together.

2 Cut out squares of cardboard and tape them together to make a scoresheet that fits neatly into the box. Write the scores on the squares and decorate them.

3 Fit the scoresheet into the box but do not glue it. You may wish to take it out to change the scores or, as you become an expert at the games, to make a new sheet.

A cat's entrance
This type of cat flap can be opened only by a cat wearing a special collar with an electromagnet attached to it. A switch is flicked when the cat pushes against the flap.

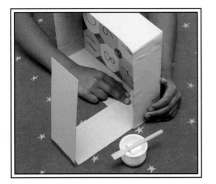

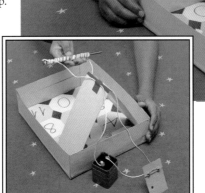

4 Cut out two more long, wide strips of cardboard. Tape them together along two of their short edges. Glue the other short edges to opposite sides inside the box, at one end of the box, forming an arch.

5 Make an electromagnet using the large nail and the wire. Tape it to the arch so it can hang below by its wire. Connect the free ends of the wire to the battery. Use a paper clip to make a switch for the battery.

6 Push the electromagnet to test that it swings back and forth. Then, turn it on using the paper clip switch. It should attract an iron or steel object like a small nail, which is the javelin. Push the electromagnet to make it swing. Turn off the switch to release the javelin. Note where it lands on the scoresheet. Repeat this step with a metal washer (the discus) and a nut (the shot put).

MAGNETISM IN MOTORS

T HE electric motor changes electricity, using magnetism, into a turning or spinning force that has thousands of uses. There is also a machine that does the opposite. It changes a turning force, using magnetism, into electricity. This machine is called a generator, or dynamo. It is this machine that makes electricity in power stations. Electromagnetic machines, such as motors and generators, are essential to modern life.

This simple piece of equipment is a metal ring wrapped in coils of wire. Michael Faraday and other scientists used it to study electricity and magnetism. With its help, they invented machines, such as the electric motor, generator, and transformer.

Electric motor
An electric motor has a wire coil positioned between permanent magnets. Electricity flows and makes the coil an electromagnet. Because the electricity's direction makes the coil's magnetic poles the same as the nearest poles of the permanent magnet – and like poles repel – the coil spins around. However, the two-part turning contact, called the commutator, spins with the coil and reverses the electricity's direction. This action reverses the coil's electromagnetic poles, while the permanent magnet's poles stay the same. Again, like poles repel, so the coil twirls a bit more. The commutator reverses the electricity again, and a cycle is set up.

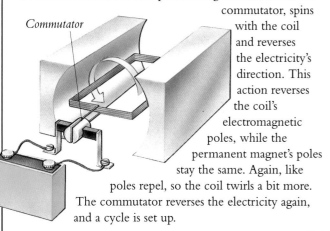

Commutator

Electric generator
A generator has almost exactly the same parts as an electric motor, but the coil is turned around by an outside force, such as a steam turbine or a handle driven by hand. As the coil turns around in the magnetic field of the permanent magnet, electricity is generated in its wires. This process is called electromagnetic induction.

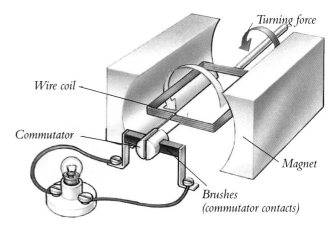

Turning force

Wire coil

Commutator

Magnet

Brushes (commutator contacts)

- In 1821, Michael Faraday invented a simple device that used electricity and magnetism to make a wire twirl around a magnet.
- The first practical electric motor was described by Joseph Henry in 1831.
- By the late 1830s, many designs of electric motors were being tested.
- The first generators were made in 1832, by Hippolyte Pixii. The generators created electricity from movement. Previously, people could make electricity only from chemicals in electric cells or batteries.

Big motors

Electric trains, such as this subway train, have huge electric motors to turn the wheels. Each pair of wheels has its own motor.

Small motors

A tiny electric motor, as small as a thimble, makes the tape move along in a personal stereo tape deck. Similar motors make a compact disc spin around in a CD player.

Big generators

The giant generators in power stations turn the energy of movement into the energy of electricity. The turning movement usually comes from burning fuel (coal, gas, oil) to heat water into steam. The steam rushes past the fanlike blades of a huge turbine and makes it spin around.

MOTORIZED MACHINES

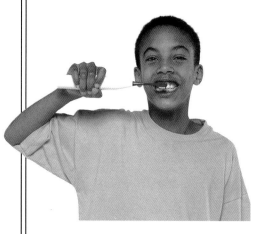

How many electric motors are near you right now? There are probably more than you realize. In a house packed with gadgets, there are motors in the washing machine, dryer, dishwasher, microwave oven, turntable, vacuum cleaner, electric food mixer, electric can opener, central heating pump, cooling fan, CD player, tape deck, computer disk drives, and toys – the list is very long! Next time you are in a classroom, workshop, garage, office, factory, or anyplace, see how many electric motors you can spot.

Brushing

An electric toothbrush has a small motor inside it, in the handle near the batteries. It turns an arm mechanism that makes the brush head vibrate or move back and forth very rapidly.

Blowing

An electric motor in a blow-dryer turns a fan that blows cool air through the fan's heater to make the air warm. Warm air blows out of the nozzle. A switch alters the amount of electricity fed to the fan motor to change the amount of blown air.

Rolling

Most toy cars and trucks work by electric motors. The motor spins around and turns the wheels, usually through a set of gears to slow down the spinning speed. Bigger vehicles, including golf carts, taxis, and buses, also use electric motors.

Drilling

The electric drill has a strong motor that twists the drill bit around so it can bore holes in wood, brick, and even concrete. Similar motors are used in many other electric tools and appliances, such as electric saws, screw-drivers, sanders, mowers, and hedge trimmers.

Starting

Without the large and powerful electric motor that turns the engine to start a car, you would have to start it by turning a handle! Many cars have dozens of other electric motors to work the fuel pump, windshield wipers, windshield washers, electric windows, electric seat adjusters, and several other things.

SOUND TO MAGNETISM

Coil of electromagnet

Parchment sheet

In the first telephones, sound waves from the voice hit a large piece of parchment paper, stretched tight like a drum skin, making it vibrate. The paper was attached to a magnet, which also vibrated, within a wire coil. The magnet moving near the coil created electricity in the coil.

Diaphragm (flat sheet)

Coil

Magnet

WE have seen that movement can be converted into electricity using magnetism. When a wire or similar object moves within the magnetic field of a magnet, the wire passes or cuts the lines of magnetic force. As it does so, electricity is generated in the wire. The process is called electromagnetic induction. It is used in many machines and devices, such as generators and electric guitars. Sound is a type of movement. It is the back-and-forth vibrations in air. Sound can be converted into electricity, too, using magnetism. In the 1870s, Alexander Graham Bell invented the first telephone using a combination of sound, magnetism, and electricity.

On the line
The modern telephone has a mouthpiece that picks up the sounds of your voice and changes them to electricity. It works in a different way from the mouthpiece of the early telephone. The earpiece, however, still works like a small loudspeaker.

Microphone
A microphone is a device that detects patterns of sound waves and turns them into corresponding patterns of electricity. Some microphones, such as the moving-coil microphone, *shown at left*, use magnetism. Others, like the carbon-button microphone in the mouthpiece of a telephone, work in a different way.

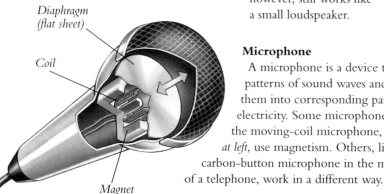

Early microphones
The early microphones used by radio stations were very large and cumbersome. The one shown *(left)* dates back to 1924.

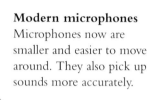

Modern microphones
Microphones now are smaller and easier to move around. They also pick up sounds more accurately.

Two-way radio
Walkie-talkies *(right)*, two-way radios, and mobile phones all use microphones and loudspeakers. These types of microphones are designed to be simple, tough, and reliable. They pick up the sounds of the human voice. Other microphones are designed to pick up the sounds of musical instruments, such as a piano or violin.

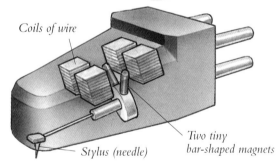

Coils of wire

Stylus (needle)

Two tiny bar-shaped magnets

Vinyl pickup
Vinyl records usually are played using a moving-coil magnetic pickup *(above)*. The pickup has a tiny, pointed stylus needle that vibrates as it follows the wavy groove on the record. The vibrations shake two tiny bar-shaped magnets inside. Their magnetic fields affect small coils of wire nearby, creating patterns of electricity that follow the patterns of the vibrations.

MAGNETS AS STORAGE SPACE

Patches of magnetism on tape are codes for sounds.

RECORDED music and sound are part of our daily lives. We play CDs, cassettes, and videos. We tune into music, speech, and other sounds on radio and television that have been recorded earlier on tape. Without magnetism, these tapes would not be possible. The sounds are recorded, or stored, as tiny patches of magnetism, which are far too small to see. The patches stay in the tape for many years without fading. The process of recording sounds on magnetic tape began in the 1930s. Today it is used throughout the media business. A magnetic tape has several layers. The base is strong flexible plastic. The magnetic layer has tiny particles of iron-containing substances, such as iron oxide, often mixed with other metals, such as chrome, to improve the quality.

Magnetic tape stores sounds as microdots of magnetism. In fact, the tape stores any kind of information or data in this way, in the form of codes, including sounds, computer programs and files, text, and pictures.

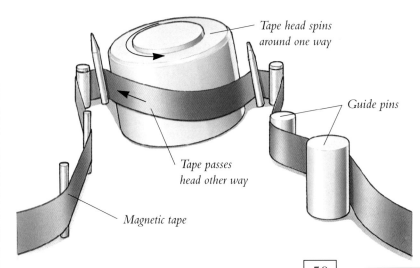

Tape head spins around one way

Guide pins

Tape passes head other way

Magnetic tape

Tape head
In some types of tape recorders, the record and playback heads are the same device. The head spins around one way as the magnetic tape moves past it the other way. Videotape and digital audiotape (DAT) also use these types of rotating heads.

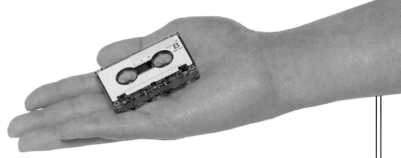

The cassette

In the 1960s, Philips introduced a mini-reel of magnetic tape inside its own small case, or case-ette. This was much more convenient than a large reel of tape that might unroll and spill everywhere. At first, cassette recording quality was not good, but it improved.

Recording studio

The sound engineer sits in the control room at a huge desk called the mixing console. The performers are in a separate soundproof studio room, visible through the window. In the foreground, a reel-to-reel tape recorder stores the sounds as magnetism.

Reel-to-reel

Inside this broadcast van, there are high-quality tape recorders that use long pieces of wide magnetic tape wound onto reels. The patches of magnetism are put onto the blank tape by the record head. They are picked up by the playback head, or they can be wiped off by the erase head to make the tape blank again. All these heads are types of electromagnets.

MAGNETISM AND SOUND

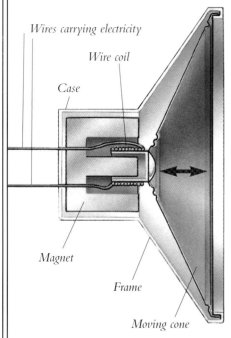

Wires carrying electricity

Wire coil

Case

Magnet

Frame

Moving cone

THERE would not be much point in recording sounds, pictures, and other information on magnetic tape unless you could replay the tape and get back what you recorded. Most tape machines can both record and play back, although personal stereo tape decks usually only play back. The playback head is a type of electromagnet that detects the patterns of magnetism on the tape and turns them into patterns of electricity. For sound, the main device that turns these electrical patterns back into sounds is the loudspeaker. Loudspeaker types of devices also are found in headphones and in the earpiece of a telephone.

Diaphragm (thin sheet)

Magnets

Diaphragm (thin sheet)

Head band

Case

Wire coil

Samarium-c magnet

Wires

Spongy earpiece

Inside a loudspeaker
Varying patterns of electrical signals are transferred to the loudspeaker along the connecting wire, or speaker lead. They go through the wire coil, which is attached to the large cardboard or plastic speaker cone. The signals make the coil into an electromagnet that varies in strength. The magnetic field itself is inside the field of the strong permanent magnet around it. The two fields interact, with like poles repelling in the usual way, which makes the coil move or vibrate back and forth, making the loudspeaker cone vibrate, too, and send out sound waves.

Telephone earpiece
The earpiece *(above)* receives varying patterns of electrical signals from the mouthpiece of the telephone held by the person at the other end of the line. The earpiece works like a simple loudspeaker to recreate the sounds of that person's voice.

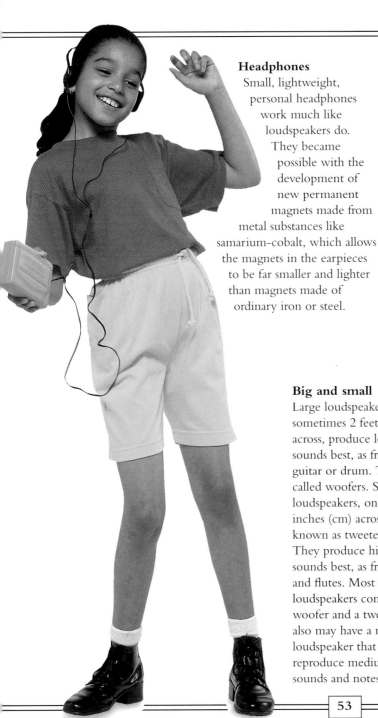

Headphones

Small, lightweight, personal headphones work much like loudspeakers do. They became possible with the development of new permanent magnets made from metal substances like samarium-cobalt, which allows the magnets in the earpieces to be far smaller and lighter than magnets made of ordinary iron or steel.

FACT BOX

• So-called soft magnetic materials lose their magnetism soon after they have been magnetized. They include the rod or bar in an electromagnet that loses its magnetism every time the electricity is turned off.

• Soft magnets include iron and iron mixed with silicon.

• So-called hard magnetic materials keep their magnetism for a long time after they have been magnetized. The ordinary permanent magnets shown in this book are of the hard type.

• Hard magnets are made from various combinations of substances, such as iron and other metals, and iron-alnico (iron, aluminum, nickel, and cobalt).

Big and small

Large loudspeakers, sometimes 2 feet (60 cm) across, produce low or deep sounds best, as from a bass guitar or drum. They are called woofers. Small loudspeakers, only a few inches (cm) across, are known as tweeters. They produce high or shrill sounds best, as from cymbals and flutes. Most stereo loudspeakers contain both a woofer and a tweeter. They also may have a mid-range loudspeaker that helps reproduce medium-pitched sounds and notes clearly.

MAGNETIC MUSIC

WITHOUT magnetism, we would not have the sound of the electric guitar, and rock music would be very different! An acoustic guitar's sound comes from its vibrating strings, which are made louder by the guitar's hollow body. When you play an electric guitar without amplification, it sounds quiet and shrill. You have to plug it into an amplifier because it uses electromagnetism to make electrical signals. These signals go along the wire to the amplifier, where they are made stronger. Then, they are fed to the loudspeaker (another magnetic device) that presents the actual sounds.

If an electric guitar is not plugged in, the sound produced by plucking the strings is quiet and shrill. The heavy, solid body of the guitar does not make the strings louder, unlike the hollow, thin-walled body of an acoustic guitar.

Tuning keys

Head

Neck

Strings

Frets

Magnetic pickups

Bridge and protective plate

Body

Socket for pickup lead

Volume knob

Tone knobs

Parts of the guitar
A typical electric guitar has strings on a long neck and a thick, solid body. Electromagnetic pickups under the strings in the body make electrical signals when the strings vibrate. The volume knobs make the signals stronger or weaker, and the tone knobs make them sound higher and shriller or lower and duller. The selector switch turns the various pickups on and off.

54

The pickup

An electric guitar's pickup has a plastic cover. Underneath are six small, bar-shaped, permanent magnets, called pole pieces, with a coil of wire wrapped around them. In many guitars this coil has more than 6,000 turns!

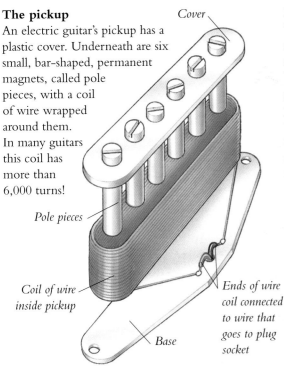
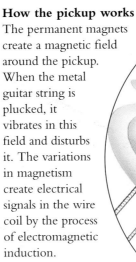

Cover

Pole pieces

Coil of wire inside pickup

Base

Ends of wire coil connected to wire that goes to plug socket

How the pickup works

The permanent magnets create a magnetic field around the pickup. When the metal guitar string is plucked, it vibrates in this field and disturbs it. The variations in magnetism create electrical signals in the wire coil by the process of electromagnetic induction.

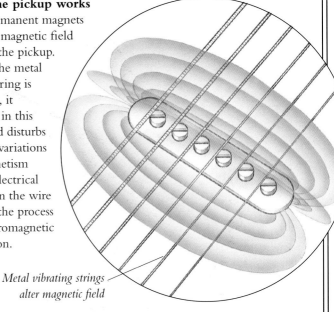

Metal vibrating strings alter magnetic field

Electric piano

Some electric pianos work in the same way as an electric guitar. Pressing a key plucks a small strip of metal, called a reed, making it ping and vibrate. The reed is next to a small magnet wrapped in a wire coil. It creates electrical signals in the same way the guitar pickup *(above)* does. Magnets and electromagnets are also inside modern electronic synthesizers, keyboards, and organs.

FACT BOX

• The first guitars with electromagnetic pickups were made in the 1930s. One of the earliest was the 1931 Frying Pan, shaped like a banjo. It had a pickup consisting of two horseshoe magnets around a coil of wire.

• The first mass-produced electric guitars were made in 1932 by a company set up by Adolph Rickenbacker.

• The Gibson company started making its designs of electric guitars in about 1935, but these had hollow bodies.

• In 1950, the Fender company launched the Broadcaster – the first electric guitar with a solid body, bolt-on neck, and two pickups. The rock guitar was born!

MAGNETS AND COMPUTERS

This type of computer disk is enclosed in a protective plastic case. Take an old, unwanted disk and slide the silvery metal shutter sideways so that you can see the dark, shiny disk inside. The disk has a layer of an iron-containing substance to retain the codes of magnetic patches, as in magnetic recording tape.

SWITCH on a typical desktop PC (personal computer) and, immediately, magnetism goes into action. The MD (magnetic disk) and CD (compact disc) spin around in their disk drives, which use magnetism in electric motors. Programs and data are stored on the magnetic disk as microscopic patterns of magnetism, like magnetic recording tape. A type of electromagnet, called the read-write head, reads, or receives, the information from the magnetic disk so the computer can start working. Electromagnets in the monitor screen make the beam scan across it line by line to form pictures. If the computer has a cooling fan, this, too, has an electric motor that works by magnetism.

Push, click
A magnetic disk slides into a disk drive slot in a computer. The hub of the disk is designed to fit over the drive of a stepper motor, a special type of electric motor. The motor can spin around very fast and, yet, is able to stop with amazing accuracy.

Compact disc
A compact disc (CD) has patterns of microscopic bumps. Like the magnetic patches on a magnetic disk, these bumps contain information in coded form. The CD itself does not use magnetism. It is read by a laser beam. It spins around using electromagnetism in an electric motor. The surface of a CD has millions of tiny bumps. When a laser beam shines at them, it reflects from the patches between the bumps, but not from the bumps. The pattern of reflections is picked up by the detector.

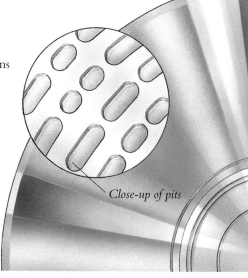

Close-up of pits

Pits and bumps on lower surface of CD

Reading a CD

The CD drive uses a laser beam that shines at the CD's lower surface. The beam is reflected by the pattern of microscopic pits as the disc spins around driven by an electric motor. The detector picks up the on-off patterns of reflections and converts them into electrical signals for the computer.

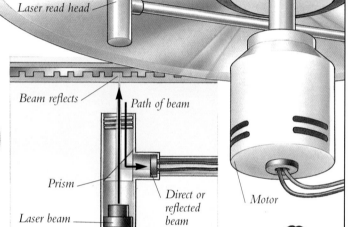

Laser read head

Motor

Read-write head

Computer tape is read by an electromagnetic device similar to the record-playback head on a tape recorder. The device reads from the tape by detecting patterns of magnetism and turning them into electrical signals for the computer. It writes on the tape by recording new magnetic patches on it. A magnetic disk read–write head works in a similar way.

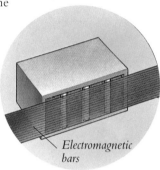

Electromagnetic bars

Beam reflects

Path of beam

Prism

Direct or reflected beam

Laser beam

Computer room

The computer departments of big companies use massive amounts of computer power to record vast amounts of information. This recording usually is done on large reels of magnetic tape or on magnetic disks, both called storage media.

More on less

The amount of information that can be stored on magnetic disks increases every year. The words and pictures in an entire stack of books can fit onto one small disk. But you can read the disk only with a computer. You can read a book with just your eyes!

MAGNETIC *FORMULA 1*

Real Grand Prix cars travel 200 miles (320 km) per hour – a little faster than a tabletop version! They do not use magnetism in their motors. Their engines run on gas-based fuel.

A *Formula 1* Grand Prix car race is one of the most spectacular events in sports. Racing requires skill and determination. You can make your own tabletop version, to race your friends, using a few scraps of cardboard, other objects, and some magnets. Remember, your version is special because it uses magnetism. Small, flat bar or ring magnets are best. The trick is to stay on the track and speed along, but not so fast that the magnet loses your car! If that happens, you are out of the race, and the game definitely is over. Good luck!

Magnetic racing

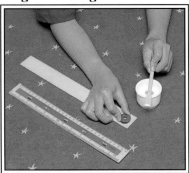

1 Glue a magnet to the end of each ruler. If you don't have rulers for this purpose, use similar-size strips of wood.

2 Draw the shapes of racing cars on colored cardboard. You can make the wheels a different color and add stripes, too.

3 Carefully cut out the car shapes with scissors. Decorate them with stick-on stars or other shapes to make your own racing teams.

M A T E R I A L S

You will need: 2 small ring or bar magnets, glue, 2 rulers or strips of wood, colored cardboard, pens, scissors, stick-on stars and other shapes, paper clips, large sheet of stiff cardboard, 2 books.

4 Glue a steel paper clip to the underside of each car. Let the glue dry thoroughly while you make the racing track from cardboard.

5 Draw a circuit on the large sheet of cardboard to make the track. Put the whole track up on two books so it is raised all around the edges to let you get the ruler and magnet underneath. Place the racing cars on the start line. Slide your ruler underneath so the magnet faces upward and attracts the paper clip on the base of your car. Move the ruler slowly so the magnet drags the paper clip and car along. Practice driving like this for a while. Overtaking other cars is tricky, since you have to maneuver your ruler past your opponent's ruler. Good luck!

MAGNETS OF THE FUTURE

THE science of magnets and magnetism never stands still. Every day people are doing tests and experiments to make more powerful magnets with better combinations of metals and improved designs of wire coils. Progress in electromagnets helps design better medical scanners, atom-smashers, and electric motors for all kinds of equipment and machinery. In the future, magnets will become even more important in our world.

The latest electromagnets (left) use special combinations of metals and incredible amounts of electricity. They are supercooled to allow the electricity to flow around the wire coil more easily. They produce magnetic fields that last only a fraction of a second. Yet, they have the same energy as an exploding bomb.

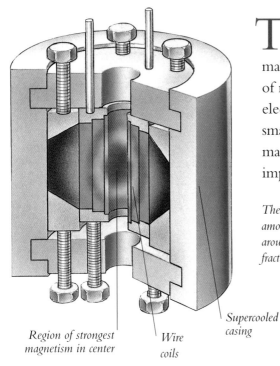

Region of strongest magnetism in center

Wire coils

Supercooled casing

Plasma power

A new design for a power station involves heating substances to incredibly high temperatures so they are not solid, liquid, or gas, but a different form of matter – plasma. The plasma is so hot and dangerous that it cannot touch the sides of the reactor. It is kept imprisoned in the space in the middle by intense magnetic fields.

Supermagnetism in wall of ring-shaped plasma container

Gap between plasma and wall caused by magnetism

Plasma inside magnetic field

Central supermagnet core

Base

Launched into space

A huge magnet-powered super gun could launch a satellite. It would have a very long barrel with powerful ring-shaped electromagnets, at intervals along its length, that switch on and off, one after the other. The electromagnets would attract the satellite in its bullet casing, speed it through the barrel, stage by stage, and, finally, hurl it with amazing force and speed into space.

Launcher with satellite or missile inside

Supermagnet rings turn on and off, one by one, and pull the launcher at an ever-increasing speed up the gun barrel.

Supermagnet ring switches on and off rapidly

Unmagnetized portion

Helping the environment

Recycling is important to save natural resources on earth. Magnets and electromagnets help by sorting out metals and moving them around in the scrapyard, so they can be melted down and reused.

More for less

Electromagnetic design is improving. In the generators at power stations, the new designs make more electricity with less fuel. Improved electromagnets in all kinds of machines use less electricity, yet produce more magnetism.

TRICKS WITH MAGNETS

MANY amazing and magic-like tricks rely on the invisible power of magnets. For example, did you know that you easily can remove paper clips from water without getting your fingers wet, or that you can make a paper bat that hovers unsupported in mid air? These ideas are guaranteed to intrigue your friends. After learning about magnets in this book, you will probably be able to come up with lots more ideas of your own. Ask your friends, too, if they have any tricks that use the powers of simple magnets to such fascinating effect.

It is not difficult to do tricks with magnets if you have the right materials handy.

M A T E R I A L S

You will need: paper clips, glass of water, magnet.

Fun with magnets

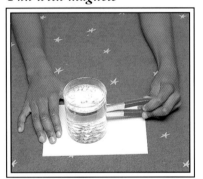

1 Put the paper clips into the glass of water. Place the magnet against the side of the glass. It should attract a paper clip because magnetism passes through the glass.

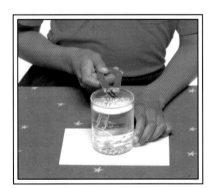

2 Slowly slide the magnet up the side of the glass. Do this carefully, and the paper clip will follow, attracted and dragged along by the magnet.

3 Keep sliding the magnet until it reaches the rim of the glass. Now lift up the paper clip. One by one, do the same with the rest of the paper clips.

M A T E R I A L S

You will need: white pencil, black paper, scissors, stiff green paper, tape, stiff wire, string, paper clips, strong magnet.

Bat magnet

1 With the white pencil, draw a large bat shape onto a sheet of black paper. Cut it out.

2 Tape stiff paper to the bat's underside and stiff wire across the wings. Secure with a piece of string.

3 Place several paper clips on the paper used to stiffen the bat. Cover each paper clip with a piece of tape to keep it secure.

4 Lift the bat from the top side with the magnet by attracting the paper clips through the paper. As the bat rises, the string lengthens. Can you lift the magnet slightly more so that the bat hovers by itself in midair, held up only by the invisible power of magnetism?

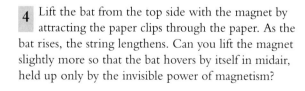

GLOSSARY

alternating current – a flow of electricity that reverses direction at regular intervals.

attraction – the force that draws particles of matter toward each other or pulls different poles of a magnet together.

collider – a huge machine, called an atom smasher, in which small, indestructible particles of matter, called atoms, are forced together at such high speeds that they smash into each other and exchange energy.

commutator – two permanent magnets, attached on both sides of the wire coil in a direct-current electric motor, that twirl with the coils to cause magnetic reactions that keep reversing the direction of the electricity.

compass – an instrument used to find directions that uses a magnetized needle.

conductor – an object, like a wire, that carries electricity through it, creating a magnetic field around itself.

direct current – a steady flow of electricity in one direction only.

domain – one of millions of tiny magnets (micromagnets) inside an object made of iron.

dot-matrix – an arrangement of dots made by rows of tiny electromagnets with pins inside. When switched on, each pin moves to create a tiny dot, usually on paper with ink.

dynamo – an electric generator that produces direct current.

electromagnet – a magnet with a wire coil wrapped around an iron bar that acts like a magnet only when electricity is flowing through the wire.

electromagnetic induction – the process of using magnetism to create a flow of electricity.

electromagnetism – the process of making magnetism using electricity.

electron – a particle smaller than an atom that has a negative electrical charge.

galaxy – a huge group of stars in outer space in a magnetic field billions of times stronger than any magnetic field on earth.

generator – a machine in which the wire coil is turned around by an outside force, such as steam or by hand, to change the energy of the outside force into electricity.

gravity – the natural force that tends to pull all things toward the center of the earth, whether magnetic or not.

iron-alnico – a combination of iron with other metals, especially aluminum, nickel, and cobalt, used to make very strong, permanent magnets.

lodestone – a lump of black iron ore, called magnetite, that attracts iron naturally.

maglev – short for magnetic levitation, the technology used in high-speed trains. Like poles in magnets on the bottom of the train and in the magnetism of the track push against (repel) each other, lifting the train so it floats along.

magnet – a piece of iron or another metal containing a lot of iron that can pull other things made of iron or containing iron toward it.

magnetic disk – a memory device used in a computer that has a magnetic coating. It stores information as microscopic patterns of magnetism.

magnetic field – the area around something magnetic that contains a detectable magnetic force.

magnetism – an invisible force with the power to attract or pull things together.

magnetosphere – the area in space around earth where a stream of energy and particles from the sun (solar wind) blows through earth's magnetic field and makes it lopsided.

nanomachinery – very recent technology for testing new methods in science, engineering, and medicine, that includes electric motors tinier than the heads of pins.

particle accelerator – a huge machine, called an atom smasher, in which large electromagnets force particles of matter smaller than atoms to move through tubes at incredibly high speeds.

proton – a particle smaller than an atom that has a positive electric charge.

repulsion – the force that pushes particles of matter away from each other or pushes the same poles of a magnet apart.

samarium-cobalt magnet – a new kind of very small magnet made from a combination of the metals samarium and cobalt, which are much lighter than iron or steel, for use in the earpieces of lightweight, personal headphones.

solar wind – a high-speed stream of energy and particles from the surface of the sun that blows through earth's magnetic field and changes its shape.

solenoid – a coil of wire around a metal core that acts like a magnet as long as electrical current is flowing through the wire.

stepper motor – a special kind of electric motor, commonly used in computer drives, that can spin around very fast and still is able to stop with amazing accuracy.

transformer – a machine used to change the path of electrical energy, or current, and to make the voltage of the energy higher or lower.

tweeter – small loudspeakers, usually only a few inches across, that produce high, shrill sounds.

Van Allen belt – one of two layers of high-energy particles in earth's magnetic field discovered from satellite information by scientist James A. Van Allen.

woofer – large loudspeakers, sometimes as big as 2 feet (60 cm) across, that produce low, deep sounds.

BOOKS

Batteries and Magnets. Paula Borton and
Vicky Cave (EDC)

Electricity. Toy Box Science (series). Chris
Ollerenshaw and Pat Triggs (Gareth Stevens)

Electricity and Magnetism. Robert Gardner
(TFC Books)

*Electricity and Magnetism FUNdamentals: FUNtastic
Science Activities for Kids.* Robert W. Wood
(McGraw)

Experiment with Magnets and Electricity.
Margaret Whalley (Lerner Group)

I Can Become an Electro Wiz: Magnetism.
Penny Norman (Norman and Globus)

Magnet Science. Glen Vecchione (Sterling)

Magnetism. Alan Ward (Chelsea House)

*The Magnetism Exploration Kit: Discover One of
Nature's Most Astonishing Forces.* Mike Weilbacher
(Running Press)

My Magnet. First Step Science (series). Robert
Pressling (Gareth Stevens)

Playing with Magnets. Gary Gibson
(Millbrook Press)

Science Magic with Magnets. Chris Oxlade (Barron)

*Super-Charged Science Projects (series). Electromagnets in
Action. Magnets and Electric Current.*
Parramon staff (Barron)

VIDEOS

Electricity & Magnetism. (United Learning, Inc.)

Electricity — Magnets: Second Edition.
(MTI Film & Video)

Magnetism: Static Electricity.
(Disney Educational Productions)

Magnetism: Why Does a Compass Point North?
(Agency for Instructional Technology)

Magnets & Electricity. (Altschul Group)

WEB SITES

earthview.sdsu.edu/trees/mag.html/

science.cc.uwf.edu/sh/curr/uwfcur.htm/

Some web sites stay current longer than others. For further web sites, use your search engines to locate
the following topics: *batteries, compasses, electricity, electromagnets, gravity, magnetism, and static electricity.*

INDEX

PICTURE CREDITS

b=bottom, t=top, c=center, l=left, r=right

Bruce Coleman Ltd: J. Cancalosi 29bl. Cern Photo: 41tr. Hulton Getty Picture Collection Limited: 22tl. Mansell Collection: 29t, 29br. Marconi Wireless Telegraph Co. Ltd: 39t, 49tl. Mary Evans Picture Library: 10bl, 11tr, 11b. Science Museum: 38tl. Spacecharts: 30br. Tony Stone Images: K. Kelley 30bl, D. Fritts 31tl, L. Campbell 34t, M. Severns 35t, R. Planck 35br, C. Gupton 41bl, D. Smetzer 45bl, L. Duka 51bl, P. Cade 55bl, S. Johnson 56bl, C. Thatcher 61bl. Tony Stone Images/World Prescriptives: 31tr. Trip: B. Turner 5tl, H. Rogers 11tl, 40bl, 41bl, 43tl, 53br, J. Ringland 51br, B. Gibbs 58t. Zefa Pictures: 5b, 6t, 10br, 25all, 31b, 34br, 37b, 40br, 42ct, 45tr, 45br, 46bl, 47all, 57bl, 61cr.